KATHARINE KILALE~ ~ved to London
in 2005 to study for a ~~auve Writing at the University of
~~ ~ ~ ~ ~ for poetry, and
~ e Kilalea lives

KATHARINE KILALEA

One Eye'd Leigh

CARCANET

First published in Great Britain in 2009 by
Carcanet Press Limited
Alliance House
Cross Street
Manchester M2 7AQ

A CIP catalogue record for this book is available from the British Library
ISBN 978 1 84777 992 8

The publisher acknowledges financial assistance from Arts Council England

The writer acknowledges support by the National Lottery
through Arts Council England

LOTTERY FUNDED

Typeset by XL Publishing Services, Tiverton
Printed and bound in England by SRP Ltd, Exeter

Contents

You were a bird

You were a bird before we met. I know that
because over your skew front teeth
your mouth makes a pointy beak.

I saw you first in Dickens' London,
an evening of frosted windows
and hot steaming steak.

That night we were drinking,
the chimneys were smoking,
and my lips swelled up

like bread baking in the oven.
I met London in your face,
I smelt wine on your breath

and the shape of your mouth
left me feeling slightly lyrical.
We drank a lot that night

we drank so much
you would have seen it from heaven.
With you there, sitting there in my kitchen,

the cooking pots start to sing.
Now the letterbox is a bird
and the telephone is made of birds when it rings.

Portrait of Our Death

There were four of us, following a dirt road which began
in the foothills and went right up into the mountains
where a little cottage was waiting for us. We were driving
slowly, packed in a blue hatchback, and it was getting late

and the rain which had started earlier had begun to really
pelt down. And then, coming round a sharp corner, we lost our grip,
the wheels skidded, wrestling with the thick white rain,
the mud.

The driver, my friend, said 'whoa' like you'd say to a horse,
and lifted his hands from the wheel. And I remember
as the car began to spin the mountains turned green,
and as it edged slowly towards the end of the road,

we leaned inward, as you do in films with a car at the edge of a cliff,
watching through the windows, mesmerised, as the valley opened up
in a passionate, open-mouth kiss. We should have tumbled in,
but instead were left unfallen, not yet dead, with the radio still playing.

The driver, my friend, looked green. Our Death was not (as we'd
imagined) the blue car descending the steep gorge-without-ladder,
slipping like a dangerous dress-strap or a crap hand of cards
flung down in disgust. We'd stopped too soon,

left still as rocks, as upturned beetles wriggling their legs,
or the roadside cows chewing slowly. The driver, my friend,
lit a cigarette and sat down. The rain looked on with big cow-eyes.
Not-dying is suddenly being very hungry

and wet brown shoes caked in mud but not caring
and the mountains feeling slow and the heavy grey clouds
like a washerwoman sprinkling cotton before ironing it flat.
Our Death was pure mathematics –

the steep angle of the cliff which didn't meet the speed of the car –
Our Death was a thing measured in increments, about 66% death
and 33% not-death (just a bit deathy). Probably, we decided,
the mosquitoes in this heat would've sucked us dry

before our death got to us anyway. It was just a slip of the wheels,
we said, a skid, perhaps we'd made too much of its nearness.
Our Death was just a minor character, someone who appeared
about ten miles after a town called River-Without-End, then went on.

And we all felt quite energetic after that. It was hot. It was exciting,
what didn't happen that afternoon. We went hiking
and found a waterfall and fell from it
into deep black pools, lying underneath.

Portrait of the beach

New Year's Day. The sea smells of beer.
A helicopter is looking for sharks.
Two men are setting up a kosher hotdog stand
and it smells really terrible.

Two fat ladies in sunhats are walking very fast.
It's a little bit lonely. It's too early for swimmers
and a Grampa gets wet only to his ankles.
There are no lifeguards yet

but gradually, people come. We sit
facing the sea like in a cinema.
Two lifeguards arrive and erect two flags
to mark the swimmable waters.

I twitch to dislodge flies. I swim
in the shallows and see a sand-shark
till a wave comes and mushes everything around.
The sea seems very small.

My resolution is to forget the things I say
when I am drunk. The cold water makes me feel better.
A wave pulls off my bikini bottom
and a current pulls me in deeper.

We laze in the water like dishes in the kitchen sink.
A couple is playing bat and ball.
A girl in a bikini is posing for her boyfriend
and I don't have it in me

not to look. An old woman rubs her husband's back
with a red towel
then his shoulders
then his old, wet arms.

I am reading Ted Hughes again
and he says, 'On this evening
nothing could make me think I would ever be needed
by anybody.' I am a wild creature.

My eyes are red from salt,
skin wrinkly from the sea –
my hair, sticky, and starting to separate from itself
as it dries.

A young man looks at the sea, and at me,
with big dog-eyes
and then leaves. Identical twins arrive,
very thin, like two halves of one person.

I think the sea is soft like a dog
which has got a duck
and brought it to the side of the lake
still alive in its mouth.

Self-portrait with Colwyn (doing the dishes)

When Colwyn washed the dishes, I thought
I love that he was made of contradictions...
His curly hair and the fact that he played rugby plus
he took photographs and walked around barefoot

like a hippy. At university, we went on holiday
to the Cedarberg. Colwyn sniffed incessantly.
I made him snort salt water from his nose into his mouth
to clear his sinuses, which he did, behind the house

and nobody teased him (though there was something funny
in the spat-out gobs of phlegm), which was a sign
of our growing up. Then, I went to London
and we met up sometimes in letters full of X's –

warnings of the places we'd looked for hidden treasure,
and sometimes found it, and sometimes it was hidden
or too deeply buried to bother with and years on
he picked me up again in an airport parking lot

and I was ashamed that I'd changed in ways
our letters hadn't described. We went back
to that mountain house with no electricity
and its gas stove where Colwyn made Jumbo oats,

thick and salty, and we ate, getting hot and itchy,
sweating on the grass, and I forgot temporarily
how the wind in my face was blowing away prettiness,
and found out that, actually, we longed to be funnier.

Stitch and unpick

With one foot already through the turnstile, night turns in
and flies board the fruit trucks at the edge of town.

The muezzin unbuttons the gates: it is late June.
Passengers escape with the wind and empty cartons

their hats and scarves
made immodest by the gale.

Outside, gulls hollow out slow arcs.
I shake and hang up behind the bathroom door,

hemmed still in half-sleep
with ivy leaping like frogs over the house.

Loose ends

Early traffic catches on the zippers downtown
The scaffolding stumbles

scaring all the wrappers panicked through the sky.
I am always late and crumpled like that

(for I carry the weight of the world and also some wine)
and when I kick the sun,

accidentally, down the stairs,
the tailor comes out sniffing for loose ends,

his *Good Morning* stiff as the brass handle,
his throat hoarse with it. This is the beginning of pavement politik.

Back-end grocers offload supplies.
A woman presses her face to the window of a bus.

Fallen down things

The hour, the day, and now they merge and it ends
with the shrug of a note rescued from the bin.

The rocking chair stills as dusk settles in. A car parks,
a daydream festers in the blue night TV–light

and the last thing to see is mountain trees, tilted
to the wind, grown tired of resistance.

The fanfare passes, the wind too, kites and balloons
exhausted, keep rising:

There is a tailor come to mend these hours
with wriggled seams of pee and beer along the bus routes home.

So many holes he sews… and then and then
wound into a temper

gathers the loose buttons and takes them home
in his breast pocket.

Sleeping bridges

The people who live under the bridge
are exhumed by their winter fires. Their dogs wake uninspired
by the damp. They sleep with one ear awake
and are always hungry and get no scraps from tourists.

I met death through a crack in the door. It lodged
in the bookshelf and the crevices of the couch.
The house will never recover, everything creaks.
The floors wheeze and cannot sleep.

Still these days, they wriggle through the window
and the blind guard of statues lets them in. Sprigs sprout
from bricks and drainpipe mouths. Who are you?
I'm just the slugs, picking the lettuce apart.

The small Karoo

The gun rests on the driver's shoulder as the herds pass through the
                                                                grasses
(the animals are as shadows in the vlei's last light) and the shot sounds

only once the buck has already stilled. Stricken, the rest scatter
and disappear through the vlei. The rifle hooks again behind the
                                                        driver's seat

and we step out. The blade slips easily through the animal's pelt.
Though its dark, loose blood and eyes stare blankly out

its legs dance up in the air. Silence comes again along the farm road
and the trees slip past with a schoolboy gauntness from months of
                                                                drought.

In low tide, the shore has acquired the sheen of sebum.
In the greying fall of light, everything looks indifferent.

The driver hands me a photograph from his last trip: a shot-down bird
dead on the road, the callused gravel beneath it magnified by the lens
                                                        into distinct stones.

I see why photographers are always talking about the light here: it's
                                                        almost sticky.
Arriving through the meat towns further north, I recall the
                                                        strange dryness,

the hot air coming off the highway grasses, non-stop yellow,
how the Land Rover lifted, sailed lightly

through the lowveld like over-washed clothes lifting in the breeze,
as a rifle hangs, beforehand, where nothing is ruptured.

Test pieces

The vineyard

My skin was too clean that day.
I'd scrubbed it very very white.

Who'd lined the vineyards by the road,
their hair combed neatly back?

I walked the fields with an old tree
stripped naked to the waist in the heat.

This is the valley as I remember it best:
slung low and stuttering with small flowers.

The surfaces

There was a meal
as basic as you'd find anywhere:
a wedge of bread

cut fat as a hymn book,
a perfect egg in an egg cup,
a salt-shaker, poised.

But when they touched,
the food moved like a lizard
and in the twisting, curving clutch

of a mouthful, laundry spun
and a button clunked round the machine
like a man with one leg.

I found this old corner,
a box for waiting,
this table, wooden and square.

The cutlery knew
I was lonely
and began to chatter.

I leant on my elbows.
Beneath my shirt
my body slumped like a spoon.

Onscreen

On my way out,
I saw a woman's body
through a window
soft as a mango
bent over the sink.

There was a pot
and chaotic, Celtic hair
and a wet sponge, dripping,
like a slopping dog-mouth,
like mine, watching

an old film
where the passing drunk
becomes a clumsy Chaplin
with moon-shaped grin
and the moon herself,

my heroine,
sweeping back her long, dark hair
and I said *aah*,
to see so clearly
her beautiful, circle-face.

Vehicles

The streets wander endlessly, wide-awake.
I am the bendy bus that flew through the avenues
or snarl of motorcycles. I see flashing-blue sirens

and signs in neon, scribbled to rust.
We seem far from the water. I miss the sea.
We can cycle down the Thames

on a squeaky bicycle. We can escape
beneath the Thames in a long tunnel
and if we drive through the night, we'll come out

on the other side of the Atlantic.
PS. I miss you, I miss you
I miss you, I miss you, etc.

Attachment

A letter leaves. A stray dog arrives
with loose skin and gungy dog-eyes.
What is attachment?

A licky dog, an envelope?
Rows of houses, or books
shelved intimately close,

(lick your finger and read on…)
t-shirts piled up, or china, or fist fingers
stacked, pinched, clamped,

bound, curling up and soft
like the pages of a book in a bath,
its spine bent right back.

Revolution

Today's revolution is just the usual traffic
at Trafalgar Square.

It's hard to say why pigeons and statues
and spent confetti gather here,

or why the air, afire with caramelised cashew-nuts,
draws such crowds.

The truth is we are cold
(from the wind) and hot (from the sun)

and the roads here have been melted
and fused back together at unusual angles.

And they are ragged and haggard and flat,
stiff, sullen, unchanging.

Potholes

An old man boards the bus:
his skin flutters over potholes, his arms flap.

A flooded gutter carries the filthy, cloudy skies
like women balancing pots on their heads.

Last thing before bed, the downturned cup
suctioned to the washing-up rack lets go with a kissing-pop.

The curtains shift, the half-moon reading glasses slip off,
the unlit corners, the night light, so secretive.

Amazement

Shoes on the floor upstairs.
I stayed in bed.
The rain. Some days

I watched it. Some days
I let my clothes
be a wet rose in the washing machine

and lay on the sofa with a magazine,
and fell asleep,
and slept. Amazingly,

my hair grew
long enough
to fill a bucket.

My name changed

His letter said:
Nothing has changed yet,
but with distance

things got worse.
The days got hotter
and the fields thinned,

stretched taut
like sheets
between the dirt roads

and I felt certain
that something would happen.
But it didn't.

My name became
Creeping home
like a scolded dog.

Homecoming

Coming back
is being the awkward person
who turns up for a dinner party too early.

The dog just rolls over
to expose an underbelly
ripe as a plum.

The walls have become an historical colour
and the flowers in the vase have gone stiff
with waiting.

My old clothes are lying face down where
I left them, having long forgotten my shape.
It's only me, I say.

That night, the locked-out dog
went *awoo-woo awoo*
in the yard

and the doors howled too
aai-yaai-yaai
with wide-open mouths

and the wind
moved the curtains
and skewed the carpet,

and flew through the house
making the pictures go
absolutely berserk.

For a moment,
the moon turned,
disturbed.

Goodbye is a semi-circle

Goodbye is a curving shape
like a sickle
or a cow's lick

or the way of ironing
a wrinkled shirt flat. Goodbye
is a grip gone slack,

a playground swing
arcing through hurt and confusion
then reversing

to the morning after a dinner party,
packing away dishes.
The last taste was a cheek

offered like a tea cake.
The leaves are rustling.
The wind has grown a long beard.

Goodbye sounds like
a straw slurping the last juice,
and the low hum of trucks in the distance.

Like we did (salt, coffee and apricot jam)

Like we did

The sea twitches. I think that's why we watch it,
without worrying (not even for an instant)
about waking to find it gone from the bay.
Where else, after all, could accommodate
such volume, such abandonment, such salt?

Like we did

It's not yet 6 a.m. but in Hong Kong
it's already hot. Birds are singing
and when Chloe brings in coffee
(she's been working through the night again)
I'm a cow chewing cud. My friend, she said, get up.

Like we did

I send you not a kiss but this apricot
jam. It's just as nice, but when you mess it
the stickiness slides down the side
so that if you try and lift it, it resists
being separated, like we did.

The boy with a fire in his boot

I

Once, there was a boy who burnt his foot.
It all began in the Tsitsikamma
on a farm in a forest where everything was asleep.

The bed heard first and the covers parted,
the old curtains blinked, too old for all this
rushing around, and the farmers looked out

to see flames waving from the valley below
where, in the light of night,
the trees swayed, akimbo,

like in some fiery disco.
A network of paths, torch-lit, came alive
as the nearby farmers arrived

armed with slopping buckets.
Vines snapped, bark peeled back,
the smell of cedar was strong

and smoke ran from the trees
like a frightened dog.
The night let out a gruff and smoky cough.

Then the farmers wrung dry their hands.
They damped their rags and broomsticks
and began to beat it.

II

This is the crippled forest.
A fire will feed on anything.
It licked out, singeing twigs and birds

which stirred too late. The boy slipped out.
He put on his gumboots. He put on his dressing gown.
Dark grasses tracked him...

...their footprints led from the house
to the edge of the wood
which was another place,

without men or mothers
and the crispy trees were a warning
he didn't understand.

The boy looked at the fire.
It was bigger than him
and he didn't know it yet,

but it was so frightening
that he grew older just from looking at it.
And then the fire, equally inquisitive, lifted its own lantern

exposing the days and years ahead,
folded neatly beneath his skin.
Moths spat and crackled.

Then the boy's flat cap lifted.
It was all that held him together
and now it blew quickly away

like matchsticks lit. He was just a boy.
One eye melted.
One eye dripped in the wind.

His spirit welled from the trees
in a clear, clean sap
which ran to dark stains on the soil.

He was just a boy, running
with a fire in his boot,
and he was lifting his legs like a deer.

III

Two fires running,
neither pursuing, neither pursued,
passing through grasses,

the leaf-litter and queued-up trees
as the moon passed through
the smoky clouds

like being young, which moves on
as a finger passes through a candle.
A path cleared before him:

trees falling, branches surrendering
with cracks and peeps and pops.
He was burning,

but he did not grow smaller like a cigarette.
He was breathing,
but it hurt to breathe

but he was made to breathe.
He was like the fire in that way,
that desire to throw open his mouth

and gulp back the sky,
the way birds float, when they fly.
Fire plus fire —

this is how a fire is fought
a damp finger circling a wine glass
to make it sing.

IV

The forest shattered.

What a curious explosion.
Grey plumes fluttering up.
Birds and embers twinkled in the sky!

The air was all around. The night
was cheap and ashen
and when the farmers began to leave

the thin-necked trees rose,
open-mouthed to a dry, grey rain
that would fall for days.

Spiders sang like gondolas
through the blackened tunnel of trees
and something green,

something you couldn't really see
through the rheumy residue of smoke,
lifted itself, gingerly, and left.

Nothing sinister, I suspect,
just a sunrise which arrived,
and in a passing gesture of kindness

tossed its spare change – crisp, cold coppers,
golds, oranges, reds –
into the black and barren clearing.

The conductor and the world in the wallpaper

As the conductor waves his baton,
his tuxedo splits behind him.
One and two and three and four and...

the brass bangs, the woodwind whines,
the strings vie for the delicate sounds
he hears in his mind. *Pianissimo*, he pleads,

but the French horn is grumbling
like a shiny digestive system
and one and two and three and four...

The conductor turns from the rostrum.
From the auditorium, the chairs watch him.
For a moment, the world stops coughing and shuffling around.

His breath is the hiss of a puncture.
His peeling leather case is packed,
latched, carted out

to a winter night, waiting to escort him:
an old man, wrapped in the wind,
an old man, scattering pigeons with his stick,

passing through the night
where trains shudder methodically,
beneath lanes hunched thick with leaves.

Then comes the click of the front door
and we hear his heart, taking off its coat.
His footsteps tread the carpeted stairs

The violins! The violins!
They had hinted at things to come,
but the patterns on the wallpaper

mean nothing to him. The ringing telephone,
the dripping tap, the crickets...
And when the curtains close with a clash,

it is a deafening, dull and defeated sound
which cannot be drowned
when held against his body.

The Liberty Cap

Liberty Cap
           grew up skinny
                   and tall
deep on the woodland floor.
                   She was (legend said
and storybooks read)
           a girl who had fallen
                   to waste.
A gawk of trees
           which grew near there
                   said, *Tut tut*, said, *toxic*,
said, *Happily-ever-after...*
                   No, no, no.
                   (They couldn't bear
                   her tricks), *beware*
 they declared
           and as twilight rinsed
                   their greying hair
           a very gentle blue, they said,
           No, no.
We old trees are happy
           just knitting paths
                   to pass time.

But I was just a schoolboy then,
                   and pale
as the flex
           of her supple stem.
                   and when she beckoned
from her parasol, saying *Tuck me*
                   in your knapsack
and tell the chanterelles
           that they can come as well
                   as long as they don't tell
I snapped back her cap
           and that was that:

32

A swarm of bees,
        anarchy of crickets and lichen
                of painted reed frogs
the forest itself, exploding
        in the cul-de-sac
                of my tongue
(just for a moment,
that somebody could feel this way)
        until a hot spring breeze
                came wandering in.

Time, time, time…
        Let the moths mop up
            what's left behind.
I crept between
        her knobbly knees
            to sleep where all
                the colours slept.

(I saw them
        through the neat rip
            where she snipped
                the sky-blue shirt
                    with her dirty secateurs.)

An incident among the wildflowers

Queen Anne's Lace is an insignificant patch of flowers
whose long rising spikes reach out
then sink to the ground in a pale splash of white.

A garden is fragile and often sacrificed. I confess,
I asked for flowers, but such gifts,
clutched in their crystal fists, are floating explosions.

I came in, poured out my fingers
and washed away the grit from my nails. Forgive me.
I threw away an armful of birds.

A light flickers in the venetian blinds.
The bushes wring their mottled and leathery leaves,
then turn to an urgent scribbling of twigs.

Everything will grow back. The grasses hope
for stalks and sprouts and yellow birds.
They must be hiding in the petticoat of sun.

How the fish lost its head

A hot wind pulled into the driveway
and leaned its head on the steering wheel.

A fish lay gutted on the sink,
its innards set gently aside like false teeth.

The bumbling pot whined and sighed
(the sea that night was a series of complaints)

and out came the cutlery, excitable
and running sideways to the waves.

Spokes were ticking away along the sand,
unwinding telephone wires, the wriggling paths,

even my seaside footprints
ran out from the soles of my feet.

Something fell: a towel from a hook
or a spine eased loose from a book

and gathered with tarnished pennies
under the rug.

Recycled small boys

Jackson, you are too slow. The boy looks up and hurries on.
His clothes smell of mildew. Until recently he'd have shot somebody
for less or, as boys do, taken a town and thrown a tantrum
and stamped his foot on it. Instead, he looks meekly down.

The four boys sit quietly weaving hair and not questioning orders.
The truth is that ladies spend a lot of money on looking good
so they've recycled their AK-47s into curling tongs and set off
beneath a fresco of falling tiles and trumpeting pigeons

forging neat paths through the scalp, curling hair tightly into itself,
these brave mercenaries in their abandoned church-cum-salon,
untangling knots, snipping at split ends, plaiting rows.
A slow hairdresser has no customers. People don't like sitting still.

A perfect love

You are a tortoise in a hard hat.
I am a heart growing gallons and gallons of hair.

You made it with me: a perfect love,
which went hard from the softness of its innards.

And though all the love went elsewhere, you hung around
like a gas, like sand in my bikini pants.

The grey fox

I am the grey fox
grown from a rat
like a building shrunk to a telephone box.

Grey is the colour
of a fire grown tired. Grey,
the cold forgotten tea. Grey is me

in the thin white t-shirt
I keep just for cleaning-up
and the dull thump of the pot

as it dropped on the floor
and the smell of dishwater.
The rain is nibbling the walls,

a post box swings back and forth.
The open door. Grey buses
and a grey sound

of a zip zipping.
An old man in a cabriolet
lit a pipe, coughed, and drove off.

A kite of birds drifted over.
The leaves lay like pavement dogs.
Grey was my breath

where it met the winter air.
I am the grey fox, stopped, listening.
I hear the dustbin lid wobble on its rim

and the cats. Damp sheets of newspaper
stick on the street
and I watch the city sit down like a drunk.

Dirty little rat

A hand comes out from the sleeve of your shirt
like a rat from the drain. *Hi!*
It's good to finally meet.

I'd stopped washing behind my ears
and chucking away old food, in case
I found you, hungry.

My smile's stretched wide as the city,
looking. I've rummaged through
my old hidey holes: drawers, tree-forks

and hollowed-out bits of wall
and I slept. I carved a fist for looking:
the rain, the walls,

I've watched them all.
I've scratched through
the pock-marked skin of the moon

and found the Millennium Wheel,
made mechanical and small,
taken from river.

Let's be gone, yes let's.
We're rats, you and I,
sleek, dark-haired, bright-eyed

and thin from living on scraps
and the speed of cars passing
and boots. I think

we were meant for the gutter
but the city's dark architecture
makes me shiver.

We grow old. Yes,
yes, I know we do.
As apples collapse into apple juice.

The secret life of objects

Overnight, something happened: the milk went sour
and the dinner party turned into a crumby, stained table.
The baguette went hard as an airplane and two birds grew
from the grey slate roof, shuddered, and flew off, sky-trawling,

wanting nothing, the way somebody who is very happy
or travelling very fast might say, 'I feel like I'm flying!'...
I woke to curtains arching and shifting in the cool suck
of the open window, the clock bobbing like a float in the cistern,

rooftops prodding the sky with not urgency, but an obscure,
unrequited and not entirely inexplicable desire. Overnight,
traffic resumed, aired socks could be used anew
and a book left face-up blew to the next chapter in the breeze.

It rained, tin, tin, tin. A half-empty wine bottle, open mustard jar
and sharp angle of leftover manchego, ripened and were renewed,
as men and women exploring in bed,
might pool their respective unfinishedness.

The concealing chair

It's 2 a.m. beneath the hidden moon.
The brown leather couch is concealing Daniel and a book.
His unwashed hair sticks up like a toy
from the toybox but his eyes are soft and sleepy-

looking. The lights are all out but one. If the chair were made of glass
I'd have known he was wearing nothing
but his blue t-shirt and beneath it, blue underpants,
and a pair of skinny legs like a girl or a deer.

Daniel is the part of the chair which is useless,
the bit which just sits and reads.
His book sails calmly and evenly on his breathing chest
but he grips it with both hands, tightly, like a photograph

or a bank note. My pen is scratching in the kitchen
and city birds sing anxiously at the window.
It's almost Monday morning, but we're not yet sleeping
and the dishes in the sink are not yet clean

and there is a scratching sound emerging
from deep down inside Daniel's beard, which is dry
and so incessantly itchy
that I should've known it was hiding something too.

A knapsack for lovers

If being with you means
I have to carry a heavy bag

with a spare set of clothes packed
in case I don't get back home

then sometimes I wonder whether it would be better
just to end it. There are days

when I'd rather take a good book
to a coffee shop and read it instead.

Gradually, though, I learn that true genius
would take a conundrum like this

as an opportunity for ingenuity.
Would it be possible, for example,

to invent a knapsack for lovers,
for people like us, which predicts our movements

and travels by bus,
or how about a helium bag for heavy stuff

which counterbalances the mass of its contents
with a hot air balloon.

Or could we develop a lonely
which preferred its own company

(if only we didn't need to wear clothing
or could stop worrying

that cooking a meal begins
with dirty washing from the evening before).

Problem is, my bag's hitched
and already, there are things which pass between us

and since this journey could be serious
I wonder if the simplest solution is just

for you to move your house closer to my house
so the distance between us vanishes.

The way we look is a game of chess

The way we look is a game of chess,
a complicated system designed to express
the way you slept, endlessly,

feeling depressed, and my sadness
and yours too, as we accepted that what we'd constructed
had turned out imperfect.

We looked at each other and we became separate.
We left London Fields on our bikes that day
and the way we looked as we cycled away

was the very complex mathematical equation
for loving a thing and wanting to be rid of it
contained within something human.

How we hold each other

We hold each other
when we meet again in a restaurant
and heads turn, with affection,
thinking they're witnessing love.

You ask me what I see in us.
We're a four-armed monster.
Look at you. You've grown thin.
I can feel your bones

poking through your skin
like a horrible dream. I don't know
what they want from us
we're just arms, holding

the way arms enfold laundry
or carry many books at once.

Music box

I had a glass of wine last night when it occurred to me
that we might've made a mistake. Maybe I thought so because
I've met somebody who makes me quite happy
but I worry that him touching me felt slightly as if

he was just patching me up. We had a connection, you and me,
like back home, listening to *Peter and the Wolf,*
how Prokofiev brought back childhood like a music box, reopened,
making me think things past might as easily be reconnected.

I know the ballerina in the music box goes on turning for hours
if you keep on winding her up
and this evening, I started thinking of things we could do together
for pleasure, for fun, instead of me, feeling confused and wanting

to be strong, and they all seemed better than being sad
with my heart feeling like lungs do after running uphill, just tired.

Planting bulbs at Arnold Circus

I stood in the flowerbed with a spade and your absence
and my boots turned a red red.
It felt like the end of us.

The winter garden we'd planted together
bloomed in your footsteps as you left.
I lost what I couldn't carry:

a necklace, a vest,
a very valuable pair of socks.
I cycled through the days we'd spent together

and the city roads looked simpler this way.
I cycled past the cynical business hotels
and the bagel shop that stayed open all night

and ended up at Arnold Circus
where we first met
beside our two new bikes and kissed.

And I knew already the days ahead of this,
of leaves dropping
and stems losing their stiffness with thirst.

Cars pass without stopping.
Branches droop overhead. I thought,
there must be other ways of remembering.

The things I take

A silk scarf and white wine, drunk by me.
I ate your relish from Cornwall, wore
your black beret, had your vodka, your muesli,
and toothpaste, and once, when you were in Poland

I slept in your bed. How can one say
(as a piano describes music) how a taken thing
looks? My mind opens and shuts,
as a door does, in the wind.

Is it a surfeit (like a lot of steps) or a bath,
taken (and when my towel was wet,
how I would use yours)? The things I take
have nothing to explain them, as a single shoe

or cassette ribbon, unspooled beside the road,
have nothing between them but the past.

The way birds stand

Why are you so sad, Girl, the fishermen ask.
As a colander drains, as shoes to feet,
as he who smokes will invariably also drink coffee,

so a girl watching a group of gulls must be a soul in torment
or lack company, or maybe a rod,
the technology to stave off loneliness.

Tackle arcs and whizzes. This is it, a glimpse of life
in a hook, a bucket of worms, dirty fingernails,
as reels unfurl

and faces scrunch in the afternoon sun
because the sea's gone the metallic blue colour
of the BMWs they used to use

in 90s road trip movies. It's truly picturesque
to feel this defeated, to lose yourself,
the way birds lose their heads in their feathers.

Sometimes its shape rises in the mirror:
the invisible skull, its bones like tent poles
under my skin.

Just so, the shape birds make
(stopped on a rock like a row of high street shops)
reveals one of life's most intimate and secret structures.

Flying is easy: an equation of distance and speed,
but birds doing nothing are awkward-looking,
disconnected, an untuned radio,

as though, without the scent of fishing boats
or the shape of the wind to hold them,
they're broken, like a bottle, or breadcrumbs.

The sea makes more sense when you look at its friends:
the seaweed, a Marlboro box, the white scum
that comes off the waves, the way they float.

The way birds stand is a way of being,
like being upside-down
or balancing on one leg. If I stamped my foot,

I could scare them, easy,
if they were frightened, surely they'd leave me:
scatter, regather, if I'd more venom, then I could force them

to button their coats and move on,
find a dark leather chair somewhere, a fire, a drink.
But it's no different in private. I don't know why

life creates these difficult positions,
but with patience, perhaps,
one becomes accustomed to the discomfort,

and may gradually come to bear it.
Let it take however long it takes.
The sea turns everything to bread.

Kolya's nails

All night, the quiet countryside was ruined by Kolya's nails
to-ing and fro-ing from her water bowl on the melamine floor.

'You're much too sensitive,' said Jo, 'I slept like a log.'
And so what? There's more comfort in a dog than sleep.

Early the next morning we went walking, just Kolya and I.
I walked slowly as though the air was thick. I opened

a stile at the fence and Kolya wriggled through and ran ahead,
scattering cows, gobbled up almost immediately

by the long, dewy grass, the mist. If there was a short cut,
it was not the route she discovered

but what came over me in her absence. I saw it in the cows.
How they came down to the fence

where I was standing – confused and crying for her
in the howling way we call to dogs – and stared.

They looked at me with their caviar eyes and chewed sideways,
as though I were something really spectacular,

or something that didn't add up. She would come back,
the fool, always did, like a springy branch.

The opportunistic lover

with Lawrence Seftel

He was the kind of person who'd kiss
in the dead spaces which open up
for a lover to be a lover:
Bus pulls off, kiss. Car stops, kiss.

He loved country music: the swallow
voice and the violin fall, the pain-
fully strained guitar, made love
worth building castles for, seem real.

Alfred

with Lawrence Seftel

We started this discussion
with me, coming home over the docks, noticing how a round
window
       lighted from within, looked like a moon.
So many moons coming through the city.

There's a wonderful line in a Nabokov novel
where he talks about the landscape passing by the window of a train
       as passages in a love story.
A window is a verb.

This morning, switching on the kettle,
I was seen naked by a woman hanging out her clothes
and later, when Larry came into the kitchen, exactly the same thing
                happened
so we were both discovered, naked, by the window.

It's not ugly or perfect. It's something slower than that.
A window is respect and caring and friendship and true passion
and not something that happens when you fall into bed with someone
       after a bottle of whisky.

A window's not a boiled sweet (it's a way of seeing
       and it only gives you what it gives you)
but sometimes things do come together, the way a sweet might drop
                from a jar
       and roll along the floor, unresisted.

If Alfred, the word, meant anything in the world, it would be a
                window,
because although it would still be Alfred, it would mean everything,
and if you could take all the windows off this apartment building,
       they would become a pack of cards.